Love, Life and Things in Between

Nikhila Roy

BookLeaf Publishing

India | USA | UK

Presentation by *BookLeaf Publishing*

Web: www.bookleafpub.com

E-mail: info@bookleafpub.com

ISBN: 9789363315013

First edition 2024

*To all the people who have brought me here
and continue to be by my side in your own
way. You know who you are.*

PREFACE

Within these pages, you'll find poems that yearn for emotional safety, a space where we can shed our armour and simply be. They celebrate the journey of self-discovery, the quiet victories against doubt, and the tenacious hope that allows us to rise, even when the path seems shrouded in shadows.

If you've ever felt lost, worn from the battles of self-conflict, or grappled with the complexities of love, these poems are for you. They are a testament to the enduring human spirit, a chorus of voices that say, "We are not alone."

May these words find a home in your heart, offering comfort, strength, and a flicker of light on your own path towards wholeness.

What Do You See?

Mirror mirror on the wall,
I don't think you know me at all.
One can't hope that skin and bone
Is enough to see what lies within.
There's more to me than meets the eye,
Once bitten, twice shy.
I'm strength, desire, soul and art,
A free spirit with a driven heart.
Purpose with passion has its role to play,
All consuming, will I find my way?

Mirror mirror on the wall,
Is it beauty that you still seek?
For it alone can't speak for me.
My scars are reminders of battles lost,
A few that came at a really high cost.
Nevertheless,
I am a book of tales, redefined.
Boundless glory, not meant to be confined.
It's said that with time,
All will be revealed..
That opportune moment where nothing is
concealed.

Family Ties

I draw inspiration from people around me,
Maneuvering their way through reality.
My father is a man I look up to,
His belief of work is worship, is tried and true.
My mother has had her own battles to fight,
But her faith in God set things right.
My sister is the embodiment of everything I hold
dear,
Her insight, always crystal clear.
Now, my grandmother has long since passed,
Yet her words have been imprinted, built to last.
The number of people may not be many,
Yet, the foundation is rock steady.
And the older I get, the more I see,
that these are the people who have not only
raised,
But saved me.

Wonders Never Cease

"Be brave with me", she said,
Waves crashing, wind lashing.
No hesitation, just determination,
Her hand in mine.
So, this is what it feels like,
As easy as breathing, filled with awe and
wonder,
...sweet surrender.

A Moment of Weakness

Lost in time,
Lost in thought.
Feeling anxious, worn out, distraught.
Ease my troubled mind, won't you?

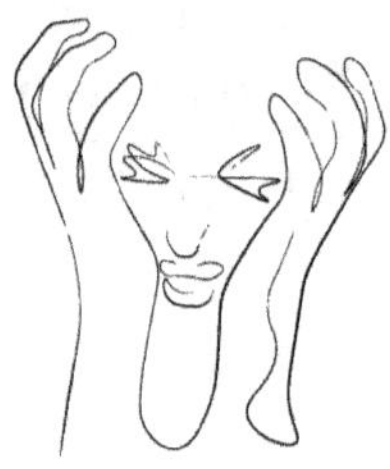

A Waking Dream

Hope feels like the sun on your skin after a cold
winter's night,
That first sip of coffee that sets you alight.
I see dreamers who perceive a future so bright,
That no matter the hurdles, they don't lose sight.
It comes in slowly, through the course of days,
And, you will see changes in the most subtle
ways.
So trust that through this journey,
Hope will carry us through.
And to hold within our hearts,
The magic of starting anew.

A Warm Reminder

Your friends sitting around the fireplace singing
songs of old,
Your partner holding you close.
A brewed cup of coffee handed to you by your
colleague,
Your hand being held while walking down a
street,
The comfort of being wrapped in a blanket with
your dog by your feet.
Someone writing you a handwritten letter
instead of text messages,
The unexpected visit of a childhood friend,
Watching the sunrise, toes in the sand.
Every time you are troubled by someone who is
cold to you,
Never forget just how good warmth feels.

Somewhere In Between

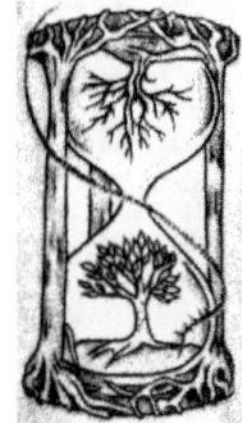

Between then and now,
The questions of what, when, where and how.
A constant quest, that has often led to unrest.
I've learnt some things are better left unsaid,
And in the heat of the moment,
Tread with caution instead.

Between then and now,
I see just how far I've come.
Embracing change hasn't been easy,
And on more than one occasion it's left me
queasy.
I do believe there's always room for growth,
And to keep moving forward is an oath.
In those moments when all is still,
I revel in its almost deafening shrill.
The questions of what, when, where and how,
sigh.. Here we go again.

I close my eyes, take a deep breath,
And remind myself that the past is over and the
future is not yet.

A Helping Hand

I'm the keeper of your secrets,
Protector of your demons.
I'm reaching out my hand,
Hold on tight and don't let go, understand?

I won't ever turn off the lights,
Or leave you alone to fend off your fights.
I don't want to see you falling,
There's so much for you to see,
You've yet to answer your calling.

You aren't alone,
So please don't turn your heart to stone...
I promise that through it all, I'll be by your side,
Asking for help doesn't mean you're losing your
pride.

These words aren't just words,
Take a deep breath.. put your trust in me.
I'll do all I can to the best of my abilities,
Assuredly, it's a lifelong guarantee.

An Ode to Friendship

Over the years you encounter thousands,
Each with their own personality.
But there are a few,
Who've stood the test of time,
And let me tell you, it's sublime.

Now 12 months in a year,
Each day brings with it something new.
Opportunity, excitement, growth, and maybe
even trouble,
But with helping hands,
We make it through the rubble.

We spend days and nights in the comfortable,
almost familiar silence.
Where thoughtful words and wisdom act as
guidance.
The cracking of inside jokes,
Alongside gentle reminders to slow down,
"Oh c'mon! We need a break, why don't we get
out of this town?"

Warm embraces and the strength to move
forward,
No time for hiding in corners.

Grateful for the time spent and what's yet to
come,
Making memories away from the humdrum.

Rain or shine,
They're intricately woven in fate's design.
It's plain to see there's really no method to our
madness,
Only that we're blessed and there's a lot less
sadness.
So, I pray that each of you is as lucky as I,
If not, allow me to introduce myself.. Hi!

The Hustle

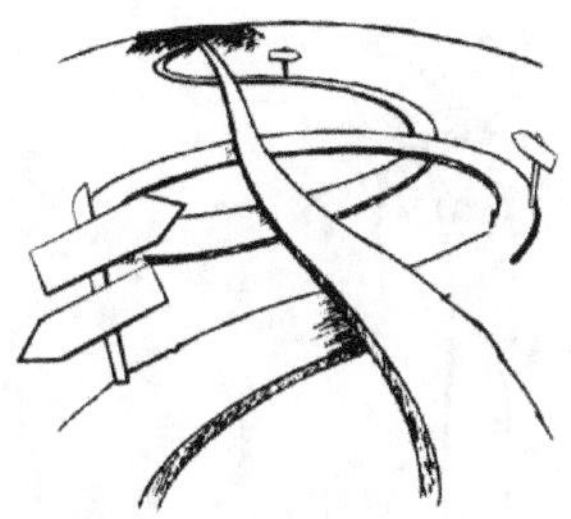

Congratulations on a job well done,
You did it! You're now number one.
All the struggle and strife,
The sleepless nights and lack of a social life.
Good riddance to those who scoffed,
They honestly didn't know what you were made of.
It's amazing to see the effort you've put in,
Knowing there were days, you'd struggle to begin.
Now, look how far you've come,
Taking in stride the times you were called dumb.
It's safe to say that what's worked for you, might not have for others.
But oddly enough you've built strength in numbers.
So, here's a toast to you and all that you've achieved,
A new you, never to be misconceived.

11:11

A dandelion in my hand,
I turn to look at the clock,
It's 11:11.
And I make a wish as I walk..
Moments captured in my head,
Seems like a colourful tapestry of woven thread.
Having no regrets is all I really want.
Heart over head for as long as I can remember,
Take me back to that night in December.
They say 11:11 is a nudge from the universe,
One of significance, thought and intention.
So, most definitely pay attention.
Love, magic, passion, desire.
It's strange, I can almost hear the angels' choir.

And I've been thinking lately,
Does it ever drive you.. crazy?

Lost and Found

In love, there's a sense of belonging.
A feeling like no other.. Home, longing.
Running to you with arms wide open,
Hold onto me, for I'm still broken.
I'm only human,
with my crosses to bear.
But now with you by my side,
I've no fear or despair.
Ah, what a difference the little things make!
And I can honestly say I won the sweepstakes.

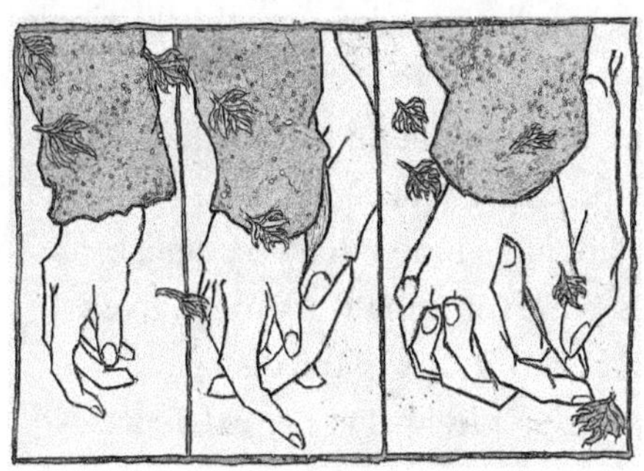

Walk With Me

Far away from the madding crowd,
I stare in wonder at the clouds.
Do I see a rabbit or maybe.. a cat?
The grass below me, a comfortable mat.
I hear the rustle of a stream,
And as I walk towards it quietly, the ripples
gleam.
Feeling the sunlight on my skin,
Its gentle caress makes me grin.
Birds singing a tune I don't recognise,
It does however bring tears to my eyes.
I see a beautiful fox in the distance,
Completely oblivious to my existence..
I love the sound of my feet against this empty
street,
Unintentionally, in sync with my heartbeat.
And, as the scent of lavender hits me,
I feel so blissfully free.

So, have you been to a place like this?
...where absolutely nothing seems amiss.

Photography

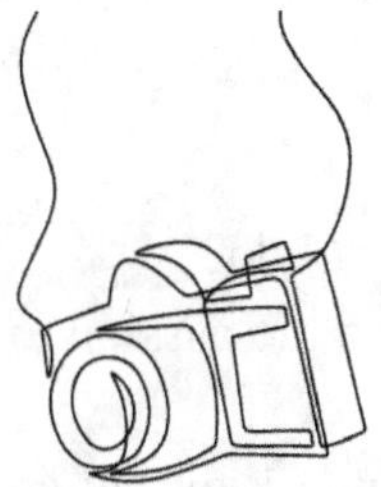

The feeling of capturing memories,
Time-stamped reveries.
Reminiscent of past times gone by,
Some of them don't leave a dry eye.
Emotions running through my veins,
Those moments relived again, it's insane.
The unfolding of wonderful stories,
People growing and glowing in immortal glory.
Snapshots gathered for you to see,
Flashes of life, reality.

The Reflect Effect

Who am I?
An anomaly.
Why do I do what I do?
Purpose, love and the passion to bring about a
change too.
What do I seldom ask for but greatly appreciate
when received?
Understanding. Can't be a burden I believe.
What has been my happiest memory this year?
A safe space, being able to stand still with no
fear.
What am I hopeful for?
Reaching a pinnacle, maybe receive an encore?
Am I perhaps too trusting?
I was asked if I was hiding my true personality
or adjusting.
Who are the people I truly love?
The ones I put before myself.
When was the last time I did something for the
first time?
When I was given the space to be completely
honest, I broke a paradigm.
How can I make the most out of my life?
By being grateful and appreciative of everything
that comes my way, including the strife.
Does the life I lead reflect who I really am?

Yes, and only the two with a keen eye have
received a memo to the program.
In truth, the quest for growth and learning will
never cease,
But with time the puzzle will be pieced.

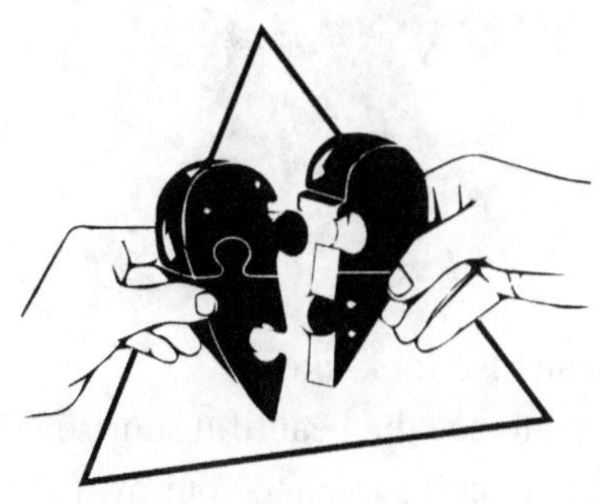

Luxury

Luxury can also look like
Waking up to see the beautiful sunrise
Being able to call someone your own
Eating good food with good people
Having engaging and meaningful conversations
Cuddling your dog
Being understood and accepted
A second chance
Reading an old classic
Listening to songs you grew up with
Being able to speak your mind without
judgement
Wearing your Grandmother's sarees
A warm comfortable bed
Sitting by a window seat on a plane
Falling asleep without a care in the world.

A Language of Love

My love for cooking came from my
Grandmother,
Curated recipes, one after another.
A pinch of salt or a dash of pepper,
The dishes were sometimes mild but so full of
flavour.
Baking a cake was an art,
And every step from start to finish was all heart.
Our entire home was filled with the delicious
scent of fruit,
Its welcoming warmth.. no substitute.
Having watched her over the years,
It had in turn become my love language.
Bringing people together in the most simple
way,
A long-standing tradition.. here to stay.

Privilege

It's a privilege to know you.
It's a privilege to watch you grow.
It's a privilege to learn from you.
It's a privilege to listen to you.
It's a privilege to stand up for you.
It's a privilege to collaborate with you.
It's a privilege to be by your side.
It's a privilege to see you encourage others.
It's a privilege to be able to share with you.
It's a privilege to experience life with you.
It's a privilege to love you.

Do You Ever?

Do you ever look at someone and think I want to take care of them?
Do you ever look at someone and think I don't have to lie or pretend to be someone I'm not?
Do you ever look at someone and think that I want to be their number one supporter?
Do you ever look at someone and think I'm so grateful for all that you do?
Do you ever look at someone and think where have you been all my life?
Do you ever look at someone and think that all you want to do is comfort them when their thoughts are so loud?
Do you ever look at someone and think of the times they've made you smile?
Do you ever look at someone and think this is what home feels like?

Do you ever look at someone and think I can't
ever imagine my life without you in it?
Do you ever look at someone and think I want to
love them down to their bones?

Do you ever?

A to Z

The 26 letters of the alphabet,
Unraveling things that are of importance.
Assumptions, don't make them.
Beauty isn't only skin deep.
Communication and consistency are key.
Dedication to honing your skills.
Empathy is an innate ability.
Faith is complete conviction.
Growth is transformation.
Hope, a good reason for something to happen.
Inquisitiveness means never stop questioning things.
Justice is the idea of being morally fair and honest.
Kindness is an understated and underrated quality.
Loyalty is well-earned allegiance.
Mindfulness, a trait that requires continuous practice.
Nervousness is a sign that shows you care.
Originality, there's only one you, make it count.
Passion, the driving force to fulfill your purpose.
Quirks, let's face it, we're all peculiar in our own way.
Real, a genuine sense of being, no pretense.

Sadness, a natural emotional path that entails
loss, despair, grief and sometimes anger.
Trust is wholehearted reliability.
Understanding, the ability to listen and
comprehend with an open mind.
Vulnerability is being exposed but it's not
considered a weakness.
Wisdom comes from experience.
Xenacious is the want for change.
Yearning is an intense longing.
Zeal is the willingness to pursue a strong belief.
The list is endless,
And your presence is meant to be precious, not
reckless.

The Pursuit of Happiness

What is Happiness you ask?
Is it sitting idle or completing a task?
Is it wealth, influence and fame?
Or perhaps being ahead of the game.
Is it a song that you can't get out of your head?
While creating a masterpiece with brush strokes
of red.
Is it maybe catching a flight?
Awaking in a different city or country by
daylight.
Is it the pitter patter of paws as you walk
through the door?
Or perhaps rolling out a new carpet on the floor.
Is it cooking a meal for two?
While looking out the window and taking in the
view.
Is it in the scent of hardbound books so old?
As stories on paper begin to unfold.
Is it your inner light that shines so bright,
Chasing away the darkest night?
Or laughing with family, friends and the like,
Yet comforting those who don't seem alright.
Is it the moments we cherish?
Hoping that they never perish.
Maybe it is just a state of mind
And within reach of those who are kind.

Now all we can do is enjoy each hour,
Because happiness has such incredible power.
Here's to reminding ourselves that there's more
to come,
And to keep dancing to the beat of our own
drum.